mathematics

CONTEXTS FOR LEARNING

Minilessons for Early Multiplication and Division

A Yearlong Resource

CATHERINE TWOMEY FOSNOT

WILLEM UITTENBOGAARD

*first*hand
An imprint of Heinemann
A division of Reed Elsevier, Inc.
361 Hanover Street
Portsmouth, NH 03801–3912
firsthand.heinemann.com

Harcourt School Publishers
6277 Sea Harbor Drive
Orlando, FL 32887–6777
www.harcourtschool.com

Offices and agents throughout the world

ISBN 13: 978-0-325-01021-2
ISBN 10: 0-325-01021-8

ISBN 13: 978-0-15-360573-4
ISBN 10: 0-15-360573-1

© 2007 Catherine Twomey Fosnot

The figures in Appendixes A-I are from Interactive video on de nascholing rekenwiskunde
(*Interactive Video for Inservice Mathematics Education*) by F. van Galen, M. Dolk, E. Feijs, V. Jonker, N.
Ruesink, and W. Uittenbogaard (1991). Produced by Universiteit Utrecht CD-ß Press, Utrecht, The
Netherlands. Used by permission of the Freudenthal Instituut.

The development of a portion of the material described within was supported in part
by the National Science Foundation under Grant No. 9911841. Any opinions, findings,
and conclusions or recommendations expressed in these materials are those of the
authors and do not necessarily reflect the views of the National Science Foundation.

Library of Congress Cataloging-in-Publication Data
CIP data is on file with the Library of Congress

Printed in the United States of America on acid-free paper

11 10 09 08 07   ML   1 2 3 4 5 6

Acknowledgements

Photography

Herbert Seignoret
Mathematics in the City, City College of New York

Schools featured in photographs

The Muscota New School/PS 314 (an empowerment school in Region 10), New York, NY
Independence School/PS 234 (Region 9), New York, NY
Fort River Elementary School, Amherst, MA

Contents

Contents *Continued*

Overview

Unlike many of the other units in the *Contexts for Learning Mathematics* series, which consist of two-week sequences of investigations and related minilessons, this unit is meant to be used as a resource of 75 minilessons that you can choose from throughout the year. In contrast to investigations, which constitute the heart of the math workshop, the minilesson is more guided and more explicit, designed to be used at the start of math workshop and to last for ten to fifteen minutes. Each day, no matter what other unit or materials you are using, you might choose a minilesson from this resource to help your students develop efficient computation. You can also use the minilessons with small groups of students as you differentiate instruction.

This guide is structured progressively, moving from the use of pictures, where the contexts can be especially helpful, to the use of the number line, the ratio table, and finally the array. Although you may not use every minilesson in this resource, you will want to work through it with a developmental progression in mind.

The last section of the guide focuses on the relationship of division to multiplication. It is placed last because teachers often prefer to develop a deep understanding of multiplication and to automatize the basic facts before they work on division. It is possible, however, to work on the two operations simultaneously, and then this last section can be used by integrating the minilessons found in it into the sections with the corresponding models.

Some of the minilessons in this unit make use of carefully designed pictures that support the development of important strategies for multiplication and division by building in potentially realizable strategies or constraints. For example, the picture of the baker figuring out how many muffins he has left may support the development of the distributive property *(See Figure 1)*. The number of muffins in the first two trays is equal to the number in the third tray. The picture also may support the use of ten-times to determine nine-times, since the muffins in the third tray (9×4) are nested within a tray that holds ten rows of four. Although the picture is designed with these strategies in mind, however, that does not ensure that students will use these strategies. That is why we call them potentially realizable.

Figure 1

The picture of four tiled patios is designed with a constraint *(See Figure 2)*. In the first patio, every tile is visible and a counting strategy can therefore be used to determine the total. However, the furniture obscures some of the tiles in the other patios, providing a constraint to a counting strategy and supporting the use of the distributive property.

FIGURE 2

Other minilessons in this resource unit are crafted as "strings" of computation problems designed to encourage students to look to the numbers first, before they decide on a computation strategy. These minilessons will support your students in automatizing the basic facts while simultaneously developing numeracy. Each string is a tightly structured series of problems likely to generate discussion of certain strategies or big ideas underlying an understanding of multiplication and division.

Using Models during Minilessons

As you do minilessons from this resource unit, you will want to use models to depict students' strategies. Number lines, ratio tables, and arrays are most helpful for early multiplication and division. Initially, students think of multiplication as repeated addition and they either count by ones, add, or skip-count. These strategies map out well onto a number line since the repeated groups can be represented as jumps of equal length, and as you explore the relationships among the problems in the strings, equivalent expressions can be placed above and below the line. The pictures in the first section of this guide can be used to encourage students to develop other strategies, such as using partial products, and

you can circle the groups right on the overhead transparencies of the pictures. The ratio table supports multiplicative (proportional) reasoning, particularly when used with contexts. For example, a t-chart representing days and weeks is a useful context for exploring multiplication by seven. If students are challenged by the multiplicative reasoning on the ratio table, each group (week) can be represented until students are able to jump flexibly around the ratio table—for example, going from 4 weeks and 28 days to 8 weeks and 56 days in one step, by doubling. The array is the most difficult model for students to understand because rows and columns must be coordinated (Battista et al. 1998). The square units of area are in both rows and columns simultaneously and this is often difficult for students to understand.

It is assumed that some work with these models has already been done with realistic situations and rich investigations. In the *Contexts for Learning Mathematics* series, *Measuring for the Art Show* and *Ages and Timelines* develop the open number line model, *Muffles' Truffles* develops the array model, and *The Big Dinner* develops the ratio table model. If your students do not have a well-developed understanding of these models, you may find it beneficial to use these units first before you do the minilessons that employ the models. Representing computation strategies with mathematical models provides students with images for discussion and supports the capacity to use a variety of strategies for computational fluency, but only if the models are understood. Once a model has been developed as a representation of a realistic situation, you can use it to record the computation strategies that students use.

The Mathematical Landscape: Developing Numeracy

Once students have developed an understanding of the operation of multiplication, emphasis has traditionally been placed on memorizing the basic facts through repetitive drill and practice, using worksheets and flash cards. Is it necessary for students to memorize facts? Certainly. In order to multiply numbers with double or triple digits quickly, students need to know the basic facts. But the debate in our schools often centers on understanding versus memorization, as if the approaches are dichotomies: students either count on their fingers or memorize isolated facts. Students need to understand what it means to multiply and divide before facts can become automatic, but understanding does not necessarily lead to this automaticity. In other words, understanding is necessary but not sufficient. Students often develop a good understanding of what it means to multiply two numbers, and they demonstrate this understanding by using their fingers, cubes, or drawings to depict repeated addition. Even with this understanding, however, they count several times—first each group, then the total. Even when students construct more efficient strategies like skip-counting or doubling, they may still rely on counting with their fingers to keep track of the groups.

Although these strategies are useful beginning points, students cannot be left with only these limited methods for solving multiplication and division problems. But is the answer the memorization of isolated facts? How many facts are there? And how do we help students understand the relationships between facts, like $9 \times 7 = (10 \times 7) - 7$?

Many students who struggle to commit basic facts to memory believe that there are "hundreds" to be memorized because they have little or no understanding of the relationships among them. Students who commit the facts to memory easily are able to do so because they have constructed relationships among them and use these relationships as shortcuts. Here are some important strategies to develop:

- Doubling: $6 \times 6 = 2 \times 3 \times 6$

- Halving and doubling: $4 \times 3 = 2 \times 6$

- Using the distributive property:
  $7 \times 8 = (5 \times 8) + (2 \times 8)$, or
  $7 \times 8 = (8 \times 8) - (1 \times 8)$

- Using the distributive property with tens:
  $9 \times 8 = (10 \times 8) - 8$

- Using the commutative property:
  $5 \times 8 = 8 \times 5$

Memorizing facts with flash cards or through drill and practice on worksheets will not develop these relationships. When these strategies are understood and used, there are fewer facts to memorize; for

example, the commutative property means that nearly half the facts are repeats. The result of 1 multiplied by another number is the other number, so the facts that have 1 as a factor do not have to be memorized either. And squared numbers are often easy for students to remember. If you add partial products and doubling and halving strategies, there are very few facts left to memorize.

Memorization or Automaticity?

Memorization of basic facts usually refers to committing the results of operations to memory so that thinking through a computation is unnecessary. Isolated multiplications and divisions are practiced one after another; the emphasis is on recalling the answers. Teaching facts for automaticity, in contrast, relies on thinking. Answers to facts must be automatic, produced in only a few seconds; counting each time to obtain an answer is not acceptable. But thinking about the relationships among the facts is critical. A student who thinks of 9×6 as $(10 \times 6) - 6$ produces the answer of 54 quickly, but thinking rather than memorization is the focus (although over time these facts are remembered). The issue here is not whether facts should eventually be memorized, but how this memorization should be achieved: by rote drill and practice or by focusing on relationships.

By making arrays on graph paper and overlaying these arrays one on top of another, students can explore relationships and write strategies to help themselves learn the facts that are difficult to remember. Pictures with constraints and mental math strings can also be used to develop understanding of these relationships, an understanding that leads to automaticity of the basic facts. Relationships among basic facts exist because of the properties of multiplication (commutative, associative, distributive, and identity), so this approach gets right to the heart of mathematics.

Using Minilessons to Develop Number Sense: An Example

Minilessons are usually done with the whole class together in a meeting area. Young children often sit on a rug; for older students, benches or chairs can be placed in a U-shape. Clustering students together like this, near a chalkboard or whiteboard, is helpful because you will want to provide an opportunity for pair talk at times, and you will need space to represent the strategies that will become the focus of discussion. The problems are written one at a time and learners are asked to determine an answer. Although the emphasis is on the development of mental arithmetic strategies, this does not mean learners have to solve the problems in their heads—but it is important for them to do the problem with their heads! In other words, encourage students to examine the numbers in the problem and let those numbers guide them in finding clever, efficient ways to reach a solution. The relationships among the problems in each minilesson will support them in doing this. By developing a repertoire of strategies, an understanding of the big ideas underlying why they work, and a variety of ways to model the relations, students are creating powerful toolboxes for flexible, efficient computation as well as automatizing the basic facts. Enter a classroom with us and see how this is done.

Each day at the start of math workshop, Trish Lent, a third-grade teacher in New York City, does a short minilesson on computation strategies. She usually chooses a string of six to eight related problems (like the ones provided in this resource unit) and asks her students to solve them, one at a time, and share their strategies with each other. She allows her students to construct their own strategies by decomposing numbers in ways that make sense to them. Posted on a strategy wall nearby are signs that the students have made throughout the year as they developed a repertoire of strategies for multiplication and division. The signs read, "Put helpful smaller pieces together," "Use doubles," and "When dividing, use multiplication." On the chalkboard today as we enter the classroom are Trish's first four problems: 2×3, 4×3, 8×3, and 8×6. The students have been discussing doubling and now Trish writes the fifth problem, 4×12.

"I know that 2 times 12 is 24 and so I was trying to double that to get 4 times. But that's hard." David, a student in Trish's class, is explaining how he is trying to solve the problem. Trish draws a number line to represent what he has said so far:

"Can you add 20 to 24?" She helps him break down the addition into friendlier partial sums.

"Yes, that's 34, 44...oh, so it's 48," David announces proudly, and Trish finishes the representation on the number line:

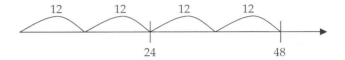

"How many people did this problem using David's method?" Trish asks. Most hands go up.

"It's the same answer as the other problem," another student, Linda, offers.

"It is, isn't it? Let me write that." Trish writes $4 \times 12 = 8 \times 6$. "Could we find the 8×6 on this number line? How should I draw it?" Trish challenges the class to use the number line as a tool.

"I think every 12 has 2 sixes," Linda offers tentatively.

Trish draws in Linda's suggestion under the line.

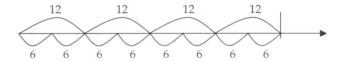

"And David said that 2 twenty-fours equaled 4 twelves." Trish writes $2 \times 24 = 4 \times 12 = 8 \times 6$. "So what's happening here? Turn to the person next to you and talk about why you think these problems all have the same answer." Trish waits until she sees that most of the students are ready (indicated by thumbs-up) and then continues the discussion. "Rebecca?"

"It's like one number is doubling...the other is halving," says Rebecca. "It's like two for one. If you do two together, then you only have half as many numbers."

"That's pretty neat, isn't it? I wonder when it would be helpful to use this strategy. Here are two more problems. How can we make these friendly?" Trish writes 6×4, thinking that some students might use the equivalent expression of 3×8, and then she writes 9×7—a problem where doubling and halving will not help since they produce a fraction. Although Trish wants to develop a repertoire of strategies, she also wants students to think about differing situations for which certain strategies are (and are not) helpful.

She wants to encourage her young mathematicians to look to the numbers first before deciding on a strategy—this is the hallmark of numeracy.

A Few Words of Caution

As you work with the minilessons in this resource book, it is very important to remember two things. First, honor students' strategies. Accept alternative solutions and explore why they work. Use the models to represent students' strategies and facilitate discussion and reflection on the strategies shared. Sample classroom episodes (titled "Inside One Classroom") are interspersed throughout this resource guide to help you anticipate what learners might say and do and to provide you with images of teachers and students at work. The intent is not to get all learners to use the same strategy at the end of the string. That would simply be discovery learning. The strings are crafted to support development, to encourage students to look to the numbers, and to use a variety of strategies helpful for working with those numbers.

Secondly, do not use the string as a recipe that cannot be varied. You will need to be flexible. The strings are designed to encourage discussion and reflection on various strategies important for numeracy. Although the strings have been carefully crafted to support the development of these strategies, they are not foolproof: if the numbers in the string are not sufficient to produce the results intended, you will need to insert additional problems, depending on your students' responses, to finish the job. For this reason, most of the strings are accompanied by a Behind the Numbers section describing the string's purpose and how the numbers were chosen. Being aware of the purpose of each string will guide you in determining what further supports to add. These sections should also be helpful in developing your ability to craft your own strings. Strings are fun both to do and to craft.

References and Resources

Battista, M.T., D. H. Clements, J. Arnoff, K. Battista, and C. van den Borrow. 1998. Students' spatial structuring of two-dimensional arrays of squares. *Journal for Research in Mathematics Education* 29 (5): 503–32.

Dolk, Maarten, and Catherine Twomey Fosnot. 2005a. *Fostering Children's Mathematical Development, Grades 3–5: The Landscape of Learning.* CD-ROM with accompanying facilitator's guide by Sherrin B. Hersch, Catherine Twomey Fosnot, and Antonia Cameron. Portsmouth, NH: Heinemann.

———. 2005b. *Multiplication and Division Minilessons, Grades 3–5.* CD-ROM with accompanying facilitator's guide by Antonia Cameron, Carol Mosesson Teig, Sherrin B. Hersch, and Catherine Twomey Fosnot. Portsmouth, NH: Heinemann.

Pictures

Carefully designed pictures can support the development of important strategies for multiplication and division by building in potentially realizable strategies or constraints. (Many of the pictures in this first section of the guide are used with permission of the Freudenthal Institute.)

Counting by Ones, Skip-Counting, Repeated Addition, Arrays

How many apples? How many lemons? How many tomatoes? Show one type of fruit at a time, using an overhead transparency of Appendix A, covering the other boxes. Invite discussion and introduce the multiplication notation as students share their strategies. For example, if a student says, "I see 2 sixes, so I know 6 plus 6 is 12," you might circle the groups of six and write: $2 \times 6 = 6 + 6 = 12$. If a student skip-counts by threes, mark the groups and write 3, 6, 9, 12. Then write $4 \times 3 = 12$.

Behind the Numbers: How the String was Crafted

The fruit has been arranged in arrays and in groups to subtly suggest skip-counting or repeated addition. Some students may skip count the apples by twos; others by threes, and still others by sixes. The lemons may be mathematized in groups of three (horizontally) or six (vertically), or as $9 + 9$. The boxes of tomatoes make use of five-times and ten-times. Two groups of five may be put together to make a group of ten. Repeated addition of tens now may be used. If students need to count by ones, however, they can, since every piece of fruit is shown.

A Portion of the Minilesson

Inside One Classroom

Willem (the teacher): I passed a fruit stand the other day as I was walking and this is what I saw: apples, lemons, and tomatoes. Let's just look at the apples first *(covers the other two boxes)*. How many apples are there? Give a "thumbs-up" signal when you know *(provides think time until most thumbs are up)*. Helena?

Author's Notes

Willem provides a context as he introduces the fruit boxes. Then he focuses on the apples. Think time is provided to allow everyone to be engaged.

continued on next page

continued from previous page

Helena: Twelve. I saw 6 plus 6. Six in each box.

Willem: *(Writes 2 × 6 = 6 + 6 and circles the 2 groups of 6 that Helena describes).* So you saw 2 boxes with 6 in each and you thought about that as 6 + 6. Did anybody do it a different way? Hans?

Hans: I saw 6 and 6, too, but my sixes were the long way.

Willem: That's interesting. We can see the sixes this way, too. *(Circles 2 columns of 6).* Did anyone do it a different way? Petra?

Petra: I saw 4 threes. And I skip-counted, 3, 6, 9, 12.

Willem: *(Draws a circle around each of the groups of 3 and writes 3, 6, 9, 12).* So you saw 4 groups of 3. I'm going to write that as 4 × 3, ok? Danielle?

Danielle: I skip-counted, too. I did 2, 4, 6, 8, 10, 12.

Willem: Wow. So there are lots of nice ways to figure out the apples. Let's look at the lemons now and see if we can find some nice ways for those.

Willem encourages a variety of strategies to be shared.

The groups under discussion are circled and recorded to support a variety of ways to mathematize the situation. In this way students are supported to group flexibly and relationships such as 4 x 3 = 2 x 6 are being developed. Over time these relationships will become helpful as students automatize the multiplication facts.

Bags of Apples · A2

Skip-Counting, Distributive Property, Using Partial Products

Apples cost $5 a bag. What is the cost for 3 bags? What is the cost for 5 bags? What is the cost for 8 bags? Use an overhead transparency of Appendix B. Show the groupings one at a time and invite discussion of strategies, representing what students say with multiplication notation.

Behind the Numbers: How the String was Crafted

This picture with the question about cost has been specifically crafted to eliminate objects that can be counted by ones—a built-in constraint to encourage students to skip-count instead. The bags may be counted by ones, but that is not the question. The cost is the question and the cost of each bag is designated at the start. The cost of the two smaller groups may also be used as partial products to figure out the cost of the third—a potentially realizable suggestion to support the use of the distributive property.

Baskets of Strawberries · A3

Skip-Counting, Doubling

Strawberries cost $3 a basket. What is the cost for 2 baskets? What is the cost for 4 baskets? What is the cost for 8 baskets? Use an overhead transparency of Appendix C. Show the groupings one at a time and invite discussion of strategies, representing what students say with multiplication notation.

Behind the Numbers: How the String was Crafted

This picture with the question about cost has been specifically crafted to eliminate objects that can be counted by ones—a built-in constraint to encourage students to skip-count or double. Although the baskets can be counted by ones, the question is about the cost of the strawberries, and the cost of each basket is given at the start. The choice of numbers makes doubling a helpful strategy as well. The cost of the second group can be determined by doubling the cost of the first group. The cost of the third group is double the cost of the second.

The Baker's Trays · A4

Skip-Counting, Distributive Property, Using Partial Products, Using Five-Times and Ten-Times, Arrays

How many muffins does the baker have left in the first tray? How many in the second tray? How many in the third tray? Use an overhead transparency of Appendix D. Show the trays one at a time starting with the left tray and invite discussion of strategies, representing students' suggestions with multiplication notation.

Behind the Numbers: How the String was Crafted

Each of the three trays has been designed with two trays of five rows that make a larger tray of ten rows. This pattern may encourage the use of five-times and ten-times. The first tray will probably engender a discussion about how only half of the muffins in the tray are left. Five-times (i.e. 5×4) can be a helpful support to figure out 4×4—the second tray. The last tray can be solved with the use of ten-times ($10 \times 4 - 4 = 9 \times 4$) or with the addition of the two partial products from the previous two trays ($9 \times 4 = 5 \times 4 + 4 \times 4$), employing the distributive property.

Windows · A5

Skip-Counting, Doubling, Associative and Commutative Properties, Arrays

How many objects are there on each of these window shades or curtains? Use an overhead transparency of Appendix E. Show each of the four windows one at a time, beginning with the shade that is closed (upper left). Invite discussion of strategies, representing what students say with multiplication notation. Proceed to the window with the curtains on the upper right and then to the windows with the shades on the bottom. With the curtains and the remaining two shades, ask how many objects will be showing when the curtains are pulled shut or when the shades are pulled all the way down.

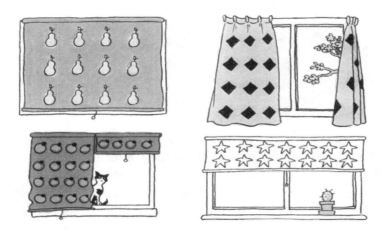

Behind the Numbers: How the String was Crafted

This picture has been specifically crafted with the curtains and shades partially obscured to eliminate objects that can be counted by ones—a built-in constraint to encourage students to double the portion they can see. Notice the number choice: The first shade allows counting by ones or skip-counting to figure out 3×4. The second window with the curtains potentially suggests the commutative property and permits the use of the same counting strategy to determine 4×3. But the question asks for the total when the curtains are pulled together, which creates one array of 4×6. Here there is a potentially realizable suggestion for the use of doubling, employing the associative property: $(4 \times 3) \times 2 = 4 \times (3 \times 2)$. The third and fourth windows provide similar opportunities to discuss doubling.

Patios · A6

Distributive Property, Using Partial Products, Arrays

How many tiles are there in the first patio? How many in the second? How many in the third? How many in the fourth? Use an overhead transparency of Appendix F. Show the patios one at a time, starting with the upper left patio that has no furniture. Next move to the patio upper right, then lower left, and finally lower right. Invite discussion of strategies each time, representing what students say with multiplication notation.

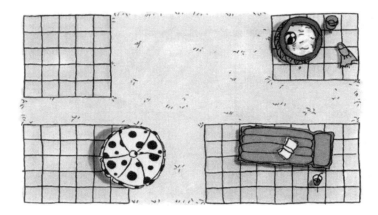

Behind the Numbers: How the String was Crafted

The first patio allows for counting by ones, or skip-counting, to determine 5×5, but the other patio tiles are partially obscured—a built-in constraint to challenge students to refrain from using these strategies, but instead to use the 5×5 to figure out the total for 4×5 (by removing a 5) and for 5×6 and 5×9 (by either skip-counting on from the square or by using partial products). The last one can be determined by adding the products of the first and second.

Stamps · A7

Skip-Counting, Distributive Property, Using Partial Products, Using Five-Times and Ten-Times, Arrays

What is the cost of the sets of stamps? Use an overhead transparency of Appendix G. Show the sets of stamps one at a time and invite discussion of strategies, representing what students say with multiplication notation.

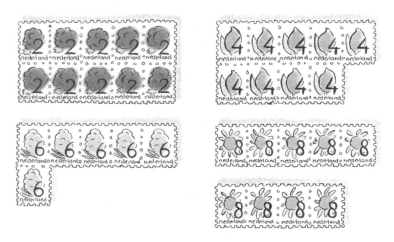

Although many students may skip-count, the stamp sets are configured in a way that may potentially suggest the use of the five-times and ten-times strategies—these products are helpful multiplication facts for figuring out four-times, six-times, and nine-times. The distributive property is the focus (using partial products such as one group more, one group less).

Gardens · A8

Distributive Property, Using Partial Products, Arrays

How many cauliflower plants are growing in the garden? How many heads of lettuce? Use an overhead transparency of Appendix H. Invite discussion of strategies, representing what students say with multiplication notation.

Behind the Numbers: How the String was Crafted

The layout of the first garden plot suggests the use of a partial product that can be helpful for the other plots—a potentially realizable suggestion to encourage students to use partial products instead of counting by ones. The big idea underlying the use of partial products is the distributive property.

Stickers · A9

Area, Arrays

How many stickers fit on the page of the album? Use an overhead transparency of Appendix I. Invite discussion of strategies, representing what students say with multiplication notation.

Behind the Numbers: How the String was Crafted

The picture is designed to challenge students to envision the whole array with little support built into the picture. The stickers can be used to determine the dimensions, but the size of the sticker is the only information that is provided. Students have to mentally imagine five rows of four stickers covering the page and determine the product. The stickers form an array of rectangles in rows and columns covering the area of the sticker page. Array work like this is a precursor to later work with square units of area, the size of which is determined by the linear units of the dimensions.

Floors · A10

Area, Arrays

How many square feet of linoleum are needed to cover the floor? Use an overhead transparency of Appendix J. Invite discussion of strategies, representing what students say with multiplication notation.

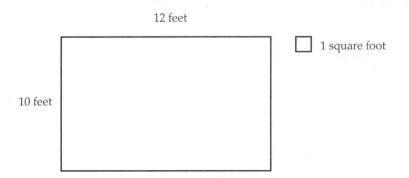

Behind the Numbers: How the String was Crafted

The picture is designed to challenge students to envision the whole array with little support built in. The square unit of linoleum tile and the dimensions of the floor is the only information that is provided now. The array formed with square tiles in rows and columns covers the area.

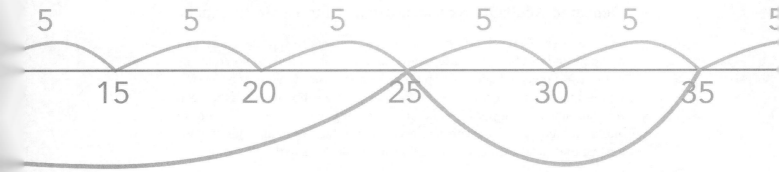

The Number Line

When students are first introduced to multiplicative contexts, they often need to count each object in the group by ones, count each group, and then count all over again by ones to establish the total product. The first developmental leap they make is to use repeated addition or skip-counting. The number line can be a very helpful model to represent these groups being skip-counted. If your students have not had much experience with the open number line, you might first want to use a train of connecting cubes of two colors arranged in alternating groups of five cubes of each color. The train of cubes allows for counting by ones if needed, and thus it provides a bridge to the open number line where only the numbers used in students' strategies are recorded. The first twelve strings in this section make use of the connecting cubes. The remaining six use only the open number line.

Materials Needed for this Section

Two colors of connecting cubes

The cubes should be arranged in a train of alternating groups of five cubes of each color (small magnets attached with Velcro allow the train to adhere to a magnetic board or you can push thin wire through the train and tie it at each end of the board).

Large chart pad and easel (or chalkboard or whiteboard)

Markers

Connecting Cubes with the
Open Number Line · B1

Repeated Addition, Skip-Counting, Using Partial Products

This minilesson introduces the number line as way to represent repeated addition and/or skip-counting. Many students may still need to count by ones or use repeated addition. The train of cubes can be used as a physical representation of skip-counting that can act as a transition to use of the open number line. Using two colors of connecting cubes, build a train in alternating groups of five cubes of each color. Attach or hold it horizontally against the chalkboard and draw a line alongside the length.

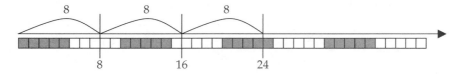

Mark the skip-counting on the line, but as you progress through the string of problems, encourage students to use the relationships in the string. Represent the jumps on the number line. As the string progresses, the size of the groups changes but the five-structure can still be helpful in determining the products. The related problems encourage students to make larger jumps, using partial products. The problems are limited to basic facts to keep the focus on automatizing the facts. Equivalent problems can be shown on the top and the bottom of the number line, as shown on the second diagram in Inside One Classroom, page 21.

$$5 \times 5$$
$$2 \times 5$$
$$7 \times 5$$
$$8 \times 5$$
$$8 \times 6$$
$$6 \times 8$$
$$3 \times 8$$
$$7 \times 3$$

Behind the Numbers: How the String was Crafted

The first three problems are a cluster. Students may just skip-count but the cluster supports the use of partial products; the first two can be used to solve the third. The fourth just adds one more group of five to encourage students to use the third problem as a partial product. The fifth problem challenges students to consider what to add, an 8 or a 6. The commutative property is employed to produce the sixth problem from the fifth, in order to support students in determining what to add. The last two problems in the string are designed similarly—to press students to give careful thought to the question of what needs to be added.

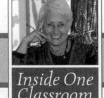

A Portion of the Minilesson

Author's Notes

Diana (the teacher): OK, it seems everyone is convinced that 5 × 5 equals 25. Here's the second problem, 2 × 5. Show me with a thumbs-up when you have an answer. *(Sees many thumbs up.)* Jean?

Jean: I just know that one—it's 10.

Diana: Let me draw what you said on a number line just like we did for 5 × 5. *(A line had been previously drawn showing 5 jumps of 5—a result of the earlier discussion on the first problem.)* I'll make a line to represent the length of the cubes:

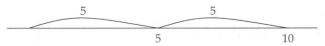

Everyone agrees with Jean? Two fives get us to 10? *(Many nods.)* OK. Here's the next problem, 7 × 5. Thumbs-up when you are ready. Susie?

Susie: It's 5, 10, 15, 20, 25, 30, 35. I kept track with my fingers. *(Demonstrates aloud, showing her fingers.)*

Diana: *(Draws a new line to represent the 7 jumps of 5.)* OK. Skip-counting works and here is a picture of what you said. I wonder...is there an easier way to do this?

David: You can just use the first two problems.

Diana: Oh, that's an interesting shortcut, isn't it? So let me represent that on the number line with a different color. *(Draws a curve below the 5 groups of 5 and then a curve below the 2 jumps of 5.)* Let's put it on the same number line so we can figure out if David is right.

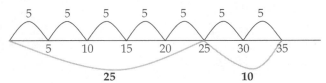

(Discussion occurs and when consensus is reached that David's strategy works, Diana writes 7 × 5 = 5 × 5 + 2 × 5).

Diana has built a train of connecting cubes, in groups of five using two colors. She places this train horizontally against the chalkboard, and draws a line alongside the length as Jean gives the answer.

Here the use of the double number line allows the students to explore equivalent relations.

Connecting Cubes with the Open Number Line · B2

Repeated Addition, Skip-Counting, Using Partial Products, One Group More, One Group Less

This minilesson is similar to B1, but it focuses more specifically on "one group more" and "one group less" referring to the products of preceding problems. Use connecting cubes and the open number line to record students' strategies. See B1 and Inside the Classroom, pages 20–21 for further information.

3×3

4×3

4×5

5×5

6×5

6×6

10×5

9×5

Behind the Numbers: How the String was Crafted

The string is designed with pairs of problems. The second problem in each pair represents one group more or less than what was in the first problem. For additional support, see the related strings that follow—B3 and B4.

Connecting Cubes with the Open Number Line · B3

Repeated Addition, Skip-Counting, Using Partial Products, One Group More, One Group Less

See B2 for details (above).

4×5

4×4

6×6

7×6

5×7

6×7

8×5

8×4

Connecting Cubes with the Open Number Line · B4

Repeated Addition, Skip-Counting, Using Partial Products, One Group More, One Group Less

See B2 for details (page 22).

3×6

3×5

6×6

7×6

5×4

6×4

10×8

9×8

Connecting Cubes with the Open Number Line · B5

Repeated Addition, Skip-Counting, Using Partial Products, Commutative Property

This minilesson uses connecting cubes and the number line as a way to represent repeated addition and/or skip-counting. As with the previous series of strings, B1 through B4, the focus is the use of partial products, but now the commutative property is included to encourage students to examine what needs to be added.

4×4

3×4

7×4

7×5

5×7

6×7

7×8

Behind the Numbers: How the String was Crafted

Although students may initially use skip-counting, the first three problems are a cluster; the first two can be used to solve the third, thus supporting the use of partial products. The fourth just adds one more group of seven and the fifth encourages students to use the commutative property. The last two problems in the string are designed similarly—to press students to use the distributive property to make partial products and to give careful thought to the question of what needs to be added. For additional support, see the related strings that follow—B6 through B9.

Connecting Cubes with the Open Number Line · B6

Repeated Addition, Skip-Counting, Using Partial Products, Commutative Property

See B5 for details (page 23).

6×6

2×6

8×6

8×7

6×7

7×6

7×4

3×7

Connecting Cubes with the Open Number Line · B7

Repeated Addition, Skip-Counting, Using Partial Products, Commutative Property

See B5 for details (page 23).

2×6

4×6

6×6

7×6

6×8

8×6

6×9

Connecting Cubes with the Open Number Line · B8

Repeated Addition, Skip-Counting, Using Partial Products, Commutative Property

See B5 for details (page 23).

2×7

4×7

6×7

7×7

7×8

8×7

7×9

Connecting Cubes with the Open Number Line · B9

Repeated Addition, Skip-Counting, Using Partial Products, Commutative Property

See B5 for details (page 23).

2×8

4×8

6×8

7×8

8×8

8×9

10×8

Connecting Cubes with the Open Number Line · B10

Using Partial Products, Using Ten-Times

This minilesson uses the number line as a way to represent repeated addition and/or skip-counting. It focuses on the use of ten-times to help with nine-times and eleven-times (one group less, one group more). Many students may still need to count or use repeated addition. As with the other strings in this section, the cubes can be used as a physical representation of skip-counting. As the string progresses, the related problems encourage students to make larger jumps, using partial products. Equivalent problems can be shown on the top and the bottom of the number line.

$$10 \times 8$$
$$11 \times 8$$
$$9 \times 8$$
$$10 \times 6$$
$$11 \times 6$$
$$9 \times 6$$
$$11 \times 5$$

Behind the Numbers: How the String was Crafted

The string uses two clusters of three problems each. The first problem in each cluster provides the ten-times helper problem. The next two represent one group more and one group less than in the helper problem. The last problem has no helper ten-times problem, so students are challenged to make their own. For additional support, see the related strings that follow—B11 and B12.

Connecting Cubes with the Open Number Line · B11

Using Partial Products, Using Ten-Times

See B10 for details (above).

$$10 \times 4$$
$$11 \times 4$$
$$9 \times 4$$
$$10 \times 7$$
$$11 \times 7$$
$$9 \times 7$$
$$6 \times 9$$

Connecting Cubes with the Open Number Line · B12

Using Partial Products, Using Ten-Times

See B10 for details (page 26).

10 × 9

11 × 9

9 × 9

10 × 3

11 × 3

9 × 3

9 × 7

The Open Number Line · B13

Doubling and Halving

This minilesson introduces the doubling and halving strategy. The numbers keep the focus on automatizing the facts. Use a number line as a way to represent equivalence. Represent student strategies using leaps on the number line. At this point it should not be necessary to use a train of connecting cubes. Equivalent problems can be shown on the top and the bottom of the number line as shown on the diagram in Inside One Classroom, page 29.

2 × 6

4 × 6

4 × 3

3 × 8

6 × 4

12 × 2

24 × 1

4 × 7

2 × 14

12 × 3

Behind the Numbers: How the String was Crafted

The first two problems illustrate what happens when students double one factor: the value of the product doubles. The third problem halves a factor from the second problem and the value of that product halves. The product now has the same value as the product in the first problem.

Do not expect students to think of using doubling and halving themselves. Doubling *or* halving is not too difficult for students to understand, but doubling *and* halving is—its use can produce results that seem startling to learners who are just beginning to develop number sense. The string is designed to introduce the strategy for discussion and exploration. The next four problems, therefore, all have the same answer. When the students notice that the answers are the same, explore with them why this is happening. The open number line can be a helpful tool here. Recording the repeated addition as jumps on a number line provides a visual representation that can serve as a focus for this discussion. The eighth and ninth problems give students a chance to try the doubling and halving strategy again. The last problem has no helper problems in the string, so students will need to make their own—such as 6×6.

A Portion of the Minilesson

Inside One Classroom

Diana (the teacher): Let's warm up with a string. Here's the first problem, 2×6. Show me with a thumbs-up when you have an answer. *(Sees many thumbs up.)* Jack?

Jack: I did 6 plus 6, so it's 12.

Diana: Let me draw what you said on a number line:

Everyone agrees with Jack? Two sixes gets us to 12? *(Many nods.)* OK. Here's the next problem, 4×6. Thumbs-up when you're ready. Deena?

Deena: It's 24, 12 and 12.

Diana: Where did you get 12?

Author's Notes

Using a signal such as thumbs-up is a quick way for Diana to be sure everyone has had enough time to sufficiently think about the problem before she starts discussion.

The number line is used to represent Jack's strategy. It is not assumed that he used the number line. In fact, he didn't. But by representing the strategy on the number line, Diana gives the class a visual image to discuss, and over time it becomes an important mathematical model—a tool to think with.

continued on next page

Deena: From the last problem. This one is double.

Diana: Oh, that's an interesting shortcut, isn't it? So the number line would be twice as long. *(Draws the number line with 4 jumps of 6, landing on 24.)* OK. Did anyone do it a different way? *(Some discussion about repeated addition shown on the number line occurs. Deena's strategy represents a way to look at 6 + 6 + 6 + 6.)* OK. Here's the next problem, 4 × 3.

Pablo: It's 12. I did 3 and 3, and that was 6, and then 9, 12 *(skip-counting)*.

Samantha: It's the same answer as 2 × 6.

Diana: Isn't that interesting! Let's put it on the same number line so we can figure out why that happened.

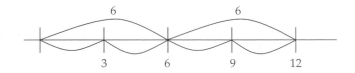

Here the use of the double number line allows students to explore equivalent relations.

The Open Number Line · B14

Doubling and Halving

As with B13, this minilesson highlights the doubling and halving strategy. The numbers keep the focus on automatizing the facts. Use a number line as a way to represent equivalence. Represent student strategies using leaps on the number line. Equivalent problems can be shown on the top and the bottom of the number line as shown in Inside One Classroom, above.

2 × 8

4 × 8

4 × 4

8 × 4

4 × 8

16 × 2

32 × 1

4 × 6

2 × 12

14 × 5

Behind the Numbers: How the String was Crafted

The first two problems illustrate what happens when students double one factor: the value of the product doubles. The third problem halves a factor from the second problem and the value of that product halves. The product now has the same value as the product in the first problem: $2 \times 8 = 4 \times 4$. The string is designed to highlight this strategy for discussion and exploration. The next four problems, therefore, all have the same answer. When the students notice that the answers are the same, explore with them why this is happening. The eighth and ninth problems give students a chance to try the doubling and halving strategy again. The last problem has no helper problems in the string, so students will need to make their own—such as turning 14×5 into 7×10. See B15 for additional support.

The Open Number Line · B15

Doubling and Halving

See B14 for details (page 29).

2×12

4×12

4×6

6×8

12×4

24×2

48×1

4×9

2×18

16×5

The Open Number Line · B16

Associative Property, Doubling and Halving

This minilesson uses a string of related problems to support the development of the doubling and halving strategy and its generalization to other forms such as tripling and thirding, quadrupling and quartering, etc. The big idea underlying the validity of this strategy is the associative property. For example, 6×10 can be thought of as $(2 \times 3) \times 10$ or as $2 \times (3 \times 10)$. It is sufficient at this point to explore the equivalent relations on a double number line rather than to discuss the factors and how they are being associated differently. *The Box Factory,* another unit in the *Contexts for Learning Mathematics* series, develops the associative property as an explicit strategy through several investigations. After completing that unit, you can revisit strings like this again for a deeper look at the associative property. For now, concentrate on developing an understanding of the repeated addition, the various groupings, the number line representations, and the use of doubling and halving.

$$6 \times 10$$
$$3 \times 20$$
$$2 \times 30$$
$$12 \times 5$$
$$4 \times 15$$
$$8 \times 10$$
$$8 \times 5$$
$$4 \times 20$$
$$2 \times 40$$
$$14 \times 4$$

Behind the Numbers: How the String was Crafted

The string is designed to support use of the doubling and halving strategy. In the first three problems, the numbers are friendly enough that most students can find the products easily using repeated addition. Since the answers are the same, you have a chance to explore why this is so by using the number line to represent the equivalence. The fourth problem, which also results in the same answer, is a doubling and halving of the first problem, but it is a quadrupling and a quartering of the second. The fifth problem takes a third of the 12 and three times the 5 in the fourth problem. The string gives students a chance to explore the ways in which all these problems are related, as you represent them using the number line. The last problem in the string has no helper problems, challenging students to construct their own, such as 7×8, or $7 \times 2 \times 4$. For additional support, see the related strings that follow—B17 and B18.

The Open Number Line · B17

Associative Property, Doubling and Halving

See B16 for details (page 30).

$$8 \times 10$$
$$4 \times 20$$
$$2 \times 40$$
$$16 \times 5$$
$$9 \times 10$$
$$18 \times 5$$
$$3 \times 30$$
$$16 \times 6$$

The Open Number Line · B18

Associative Property, Doubling and Halving

See B16 for details (page 30).

$$12 \times 10$$
$$6 \times 20$$
$$3 \times 40$$
$$15 \times 8$$
$$30 \times 4$$
$$60 \times 2$$
$$120 \times 1$$
$$18 \times 3$$

Cars	1	2	4	5
Tires	4	8	16	20

The Ratio Table

As students appear to become comfortable with the number line and the use of partial products, you can begin to use the ratio table to support multiplicative thinking. The table can be drawn as above, or you may prefer to use a t-chart. Stay in the context by talking about cars and tires, or juice boxes and six-packs, to help students realize the mathematical meaning of what they are doing. Remember that students can fall back on the use of repeated addition if necessary.

Materials Needed for this Section

Large chart pad and easel (or chalkboard or whiteboard)

Markers

Distributive Property, Doubling, Using Partial Products, Proportional Reasoning

This string of related problems is designed to encourage students to use multiplication facts they know in order to find answers to other, more challenging ones. It is assumed that your students have not yet automatized the multiplication facts, so these strings are designed to help them do so by focusing on number relationships. Do one problem at a time, giving students some think time before you start discussion. Presenting the problems in this string in a context, such as a number of cars and a number of tires, helps students realize the meaning of what they are doing. The ratio table is a good model for illustrating such a context. Here it is represented as a t-chart.

Number of Cars	Number of Tires
1	4
2	8
4	

2 × 4
4 × 4
8 × 4
10 × 4
9 × 4
12 × 4
5 × 4
6 × 4

Behind the Numbers: How the String was Crafted

The problems in this string have been chosen to encourage students to use facts they know as helper partial products in solving more difficult problems. The big idea underlying this strategy is the distributive property. The first problem will probably be easy for your students. Even if they don't know the answer automatically, they can use addition. The first product can now be used to solve the second problem. Some students may still need to think of this as repeated addition, 4 + 4 + 4 + 4. Some may even still need to use their fingers. The string is designed to encourage the use of more efficient strategies, so ask students to share a few. If no one has thought to use the first problem to solve the second, encourage them to consider how it might be helpful—how 4 × 4 = 2 × 2 × 4. The third problem may be more difficult, but the product of the second problem can now be used to solve it because one of the factors, 8, is double one of the factors in the previous problems. The fourth problem may be easy if students know the pattern of multiplication by ten. If a student says, "I just added a zero," encourage the class to recognize that writing a zero down is not adding, since 4 + 0 = 4, not 40. Encourage them to realize that 10 × 4 is equivalent to 4 × 10 (which means that there are 4 tens; hence the zero is placed to move the 4 over to the tens place). Other students may not know about the place value pattern that results when multiplying by ten, but they may think to add the products of the first and third problems in the string. Adding the products of these problems also produces 10 groups of four. Similarly, the next three problems can be solved by using others in the string. For example, 5 × 4 can be solved by halving the product of 10 × 4. The last problem can be solved by adding another group of four to the product of the previous problem.

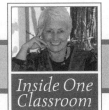

Inside One Classroom

A Portion of the Minilesson

Margie (the teacher): Here's our first one. *(Writes 2 × 4)*. Let's try thinking about this as 2 cars, 4 tires on each one. How many tires? Jamie?

Jamie: Eight. Because 4 + 4 is 8.

Margie: That was an easy one, wasn't it. I'm going to record on a t-chart today. *(Draws a t-chart as follows)*:

Number of Cars	Number of Tires
2	8

OK. Here's the next one. How about 4 cars? *(Writes 4 × 4)*. How many tires? Rico?

Rico: It's twice as many. Sixteen.

Margie: *(Records the strategy on the t-chart)*

Number of Cars	Number of Tires
×2 ⟨ 2	8 ⟩
4	16 ⟩ ×2

That was a fast way! Turn to the person sitting next to you and discuss what Rico did. See if you can explain to each other why it worked.

Author's Notes

Margie places the problems in context to help students realize what they are doing. The shift from repeated addition to multiplicative thinking based on proportional reasoning can be difficult.

The proportional reasoning (×2) is also recorded and students are provided with pair talk time to make sense of this for themselves.

Cars and Tires · C2

Distributive Property, Doubling, Using Partial Products, Proportional Reasoning

This string is similar to C1. It is designed to encourage students to use multiplication facts they know in order to find answers to other, more challenging ones. Refer to C1 and Inside the Classroom, pages 34–35, for further information.

Number of Cars	Number of Tires
1	4
3	12
6	24

3 × 4
6 × 4
12 × 4
10 × 4
11 × 4
9 × 4
5 × 4

Behind the Numbers: How the String was Crafted

The problems in this string have been chosen to encourage students to use facts they know as helper partial products in solving more difficult problems. The first problem will probably be easy for your students. Even if they don't know the answer automatically, they can use addition. The first product can now be used to solve the second problem by doubling the 3. Some students may still need to think of this as repeated addition. Some may even still need to use their fingers. If no one has thought to use the first problem to solve the second, encourage them to consider how it might be helpful—how $6 \times 4 = 2 \times 3 \times 4$. The third problem may be more difficult, but the product of the second problem can now be used to solve it. The fourth problem may be easy if students know the pattern of multiplication by ten. The last problem can be solved by halving the product of 10×4. See C3 for additional support.

Cars and Tires · C3

Distributive Property, Doubling, Using Partial Products, Proportional Reasoning

See C2 for details (above).

Number of Cars	Number of Tires
1	4
4	8
8	32

4 × 4
8 × 4
16 × 4
20 × 4
19 × 4
21 × 4
15 × 4

Distributive Property, Doubling, Using Partial Products, Proportional Reasoning

This string of related problems is designed to encourage students to use multiplication facts they know as helper partial products to find the answers to other, more difficult problems. Do one problem at a time and record students' strategies on a t-chart. Presenting the problems in this string in a context, such as six-packs of juice, will help students realize the meaning of what they are doing.

Number of Packs	Number of Juice Boxes
1	6
2	12

2×6

4×6

6×6

8×6

10×6

9×6

12×6

Behind the Numbers: How the String was Crafted

The product of the second problem is double the value of the product of the first, and the first two problems can be used to solve the third. The fourth product is double the value of the second, and can also be solved with the partial products of the first and third. Then, 9×6 appears after 10×6 to encourage students to use the ten-times strategy for the nine-times table (subtracting one group of six). The last problem can be solved in many ways with a variety of partial products on the chart. This string is designed to help students automatize the multiplication facts by focusing on relationships. The big idea underlying this strategy is the distributive property. As you proceed with the string encourage students to look for relationships and use them. When needed, draw representations of the juice boxes or use repeated addition, circling the groups (as shown below), to help students who are struggling to envision the partial products.

$$8 \times 6 = (4 \times 6) + (4 \times 6) = (6 \times 6) + (2 \times 6)$$

$$(6 + 6 + 6 + 6) + (6 + 6 + 6 + 6)$$

$$(6 + 6 + 6 + 6 + 6 + 6) + (6 + 6)$$

For additional support, see the related strings that follow—C5 and C6.

Juice Boxes and Six-Packs · C5

Distributive Property, Doubling, Using Partial Products, Proportional Reasoning

See C4 for details (page 37).

Number of Packs	Number of Juice Boxes
1	6
3	18

3×6

6×6

7×6

9×6

12×6

10×6

11×6

15×6

Juice Boxes and Six-Packs · C6

Distributive Property, Doubling, Using Partial Products, Proportional Reasoning

See C4 for details (page 37).

5×6

10×6

15×6

9×6

4×6

8×6

20×6

The Cost of Tickets · C7

Distributive Property, Doubling, Using Partial Products, Proportional Reasoning

This string of related problems is designed to encourage students to use multiplication facts they know as helper partial products in solving more difficult problems. You might use the context of buying a number of tickets that cost $7.00 each. Do one problem at a time and encourage students to use the first few problems in the string to solve the later ones. Model students' ideas on a t-chart, or record their repeated addition and group the factors as appropriate to represent their strategies.

Number of Tickets	Cost
1	7
2	14
4	28

2×7

4×7

8×7

10×7

9×7

12×7

6×7

Behind the Numbers: How the String was Crafted

The value of the product to the second problem is double that of the first. The product of the third problem is double the value of the second. Ten groups of seven can be made with 2 groups of seven and 8 groups of seven. Nine groups of seven is one group less than 10 groups of seven. The big idea underlying this strategy is the distributive property. As the string progresses, students will need to examine the numbers and find the partial products that can be helpful. For additional support, see the related strings that follow—C8 and C9.

The Cost of Tickets · C8

Distributive Property, Doubling, Using Partial Products, Proportional Reasoning

See C7 for details (above).

Number of Tickets	Cost
1	7
2	14
3	21
6	42

2×7

3×7

6×7

9×7

10×7

11×7

5×7

The Cost of Tickets · C9

Distributive Property, Doubling, Using Partial Products, Ratio Table

See C7 for details (page 38).

Number of Tickets	Cost
1	7
5	35
10	70
20	140

5 × 7

10 × 7

20 × 7

9 × 7

6 × 7

11 × 7

Days and Weeks · C10

Distributive Property, Doubling, Using Partial Products, Proportional Reasoning

This string of related problems is designed to encourage students to use multiplication facts they know as helper partial products in solving more difficult problems. With this string, you might use the context of the number of days contained in a certain number of weeks. Do one problem at a time and encourage students to use the first few problems in the string to solve the later ones. Model students' ideas on a t-chart, or record their repeated addition and group the factors as appropriate to represent their strategies.

Number of Weeks	Number of Days
1	7
2	14
4	28
5	35

2 × 7

4 × 7

5 × 7

3 × 7

7 × 7

9 × 7

11 × 7

6 × 7

$$5 \times 7 = (4 = 7) + (1 \times 7)$$
$$\boxed{(7 + 7 + 7 + 7)} \quad + \quad \boxed{(7)}$$

Behind the Numbers: How the String was Crafted

The product of the second problem is double that of the first. The third problem adds just one more group of seven. The fourth problem challenges students to think about adding or removing a group (using either the first or the second problem). The fifth problem can be solved with the partial products of the first and third, or the second and fourth, problems. The remaining problems in this string can be solved using a variety of partial products from the earlier problems. The strategy of using partial products is based on the distributive property. For additional support, see the related strings that follow—C11 and C12.

Days and Weeks · C11

Distributive Property, Doubling, Using Partial Products, Proportional Reasoning

See C10 for details (page 40).

Number of Weeks	Number of Days
1	7
3	21
6	42

3×7

6×7

5×7

8×7

11×7

9×7

Days and Weeks · C12

Distributive Property, Doubling, Using Partial Products, Proportional Reasoning

See C10 for details (page 40).

Number of Weeks	Number of Days
1	7
2	14
5	35

2×7

5×7

10×7

9×7

11×7

6×7

4×7

14×7

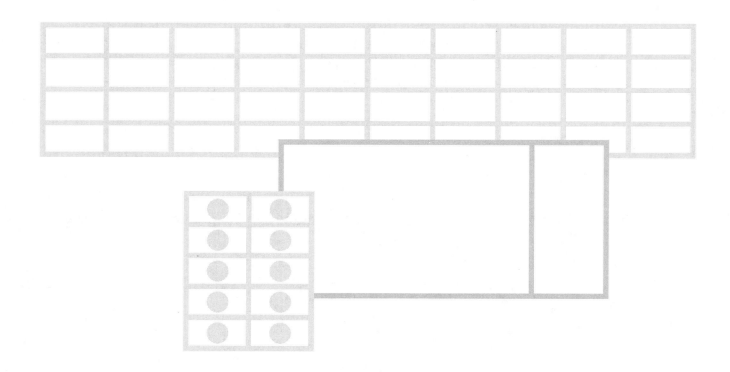

Arrays

Arrays can be very helpful geometric models for exploring the relationship between multiplication and division. This section is progressive. Initially quick images with ten-frames—arrays of dots—are used to encourage students to use partial products to calculate the total number of elements in the array. Because the images are shown only briefly, it is not possible for students to count each dot in order to find the total. Later in this section, trains of connecting cubes are used. A rectangle drawn on graph paper is used as a representation of the trains, as a bridge to introduce students to the open array—the primary model used in later work. The last several minilessons in this section make use of an open array only to represent students' strategies.

Materials Needed for this Section

Overhead projector

Overhead transparencies of Appendix K

Connecting cubes

Chart-size graph paper

Markers

Using Five-Times, Using Partial Products, Doubling

This string of quick images is designed to encourage students to use partial products to find the total number of elements of larger arrays. Using cut out transparencies from Appendix K show one image at a time briefly and then turn off the light on the projector or cover the image as you ask students to determine how many dots there are and to share how they know. As you use the 2 × 5 and 1 × 5 arrays to make the other images, leave a slight space between them to enable students to see them easily. To record the strategies draw an outline and label the dimensions. For example, if a student says for the third problem, "I saw two 2 by 5 boxes. I knew that was 10 and 10…so 20," use the quick image shown to highlight the strategy and draw an outline, labeling the dimensions as shown below. Be sure to indicate (or ask) where the 10 is and what the dimensions of the new array would be (2 × 5 + 2 × 5 = 4 × 5).

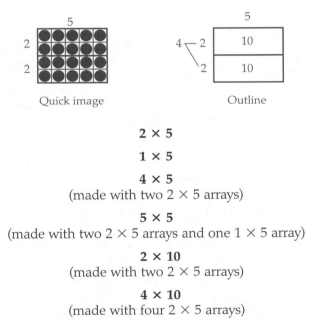

Quick image   Outline

2 × 5

1 × 5

4 × 5
(made with two 2 × 5 arrays)

5 × 5
(made with two 2 × 5 arrays and one 1 × 5 array)

2 × 10
(made with two 2 × 5 arrays)

4 × 10
(made with four 2 × 5 arrays)

Behind the Numbers: How the String was Crafted

The numbers in the string were chosen to continue to develop the idea that small arrays can be used to build larger arrays and that the total number of elements in an array can be determined with multiplication (number of rows × number of columns). Only two small arrays are used, a 2 × 5 and a 1 × 5; using only two makes it more likely that students will be able to determine the sizes shown (since they are seen only briefly). The quick image technique is used to encourage students to move away from counting each dot, and to begin to consider other strategies, such as doubling and/or using partial products of five-times and ten-times.

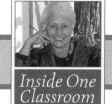
Toni (the teacher): I'm going to flash the image quickly. At the count of three, 1, 2, 3. *(Flashes the image.)* OK, thumbs-up when you're ready to share. Tanisha?

Tanisha: It was 20 altogether.

Toni: And how did you know that?

Tanisha: I saw two 2 by 5s, but they were put together differently than before. The other array—the 4 by 5—was almost a square. This one was different—it was a long rectangle.

Toni: It might help to think about the dimensions of this long rectangle.

Tanisha: I think it might be a 2 by 10. The short side was 2 and the long side was 10 because 5 and 5 makes 10.

Toni: So here's the quick image I showed you. *(Puts the image on the overhead and records an outline labeling the dimensions.)*

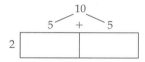

Author's Notes

Toni prepares the students for the quick image by counting to three. This ensures that everyone is ready.

Toni supports communication by asking the student to explain her thinking.

Toni shows respect for the student's ideas by using her language ("a long rectangle"), but still pushes her to be more explicit.

Toni labels the dimensions on the overhead outline as a tool to communicate Tanisha's strategy. She also checks for understanding in the other students by asking them what the dimensions of the new array would be.

Quick Image Arrays · D2

Using Five-Times, Using Partial Products, Doubling

As with D1, this string of quick images is designed to encourage students to use partial products to find the products of larger arrays. Using cut out transparencies from Appendix K show one image at a time briefly and then turn off the light on the projector or cover the image as you ask students to determine how many dots there are, and to share how they know. As you use the 2×5 and 1×5 to make the other images, leave a slight space between them to enable students to see them easily. Record the strategy on an outline of the image and label the dimensions as students describe their strategies. See Inside One Classroom (above), for further details.

2 × 5

1 × 5

3 × 5
(made with one 1×5 array and one 2×5 array)

5 × 5
(made with two 2×5 arrays and one 1×5 array)

4 × 5
(made with two 2×5 arrays)

2 × 10
(made with two 2×5 arrays)

Behind the Numbers: How the String was Crafted

This string was designed similarly to D1. The numbers were chosen to develop the idea that small arrays can be used to build larger arrays. The third problem can be solved using the first two problems. The fourth can be solved with the first and the third, etc. Only two small arrays are used, a 2 × 5 and a 1 × 5; using only two makes it more likely that students will be able to determine the sizes shown (since they are seen only briefly). The quick image technique is used to encourage students to move away from counting each dot and to begin to consider other strategies, such as doubling and/or using partial products of five-times and ten-times. See D3 for additional support.

Quick Image Arrays · D3

Using Five-Times, Using Partial Products, Doubling

See D2 for details (page 44).

2 × 5

1 × 5

3 × 5
(made with one 2 × 5 array and one 1 × 5 array)

5 × 4
(made with two 2 × 5 arrays oriented vertically,
so that 5 rows and 4 columns are shown)

4 × 5
(turn the previous array horizontally)

5 × 5
(made with two 2 × 5 arrays and one 1 × 5 array)

Arrays with Connecting Cubes · D4

Distributive and Commutative Properties, Using Ten-Times, Using Partial Products

This string of related problems is designed to encourage students to use the distributive property of multiplication over subtraction, specifically to use the product of ten-times to figure out the product of nine-times. Do one problem at a time. Use connecting cubes to make towers as a visual representation while you discuss students' strategies. For example, for 10 × 4, make four towers of ten cubes each. Also make a 10 × 4 rectangle on graph paper as a representation, explaining that it also shows ten rows of four. Many students may say about the first problem, "I just added a zero." To help them recognize that writing a zero down is not adding, write $4 + 0 = 4$ and ask, "How did you get forty? Did you really add a zero? Forty has four tens, doesn't it? Can we find them?" Help them realize that the 10×4 array you have made can be rotated to show that 10×4 is equivalent to 4×10 (which means that there are 4 tens, so the zero is written in the ones place and the 4 is moved to the tens place). Two big ideas underlie this discussion: the commutative property and multiplication by ten. The second problem in the string will help you develop these ideas if no one says, "I added a zero."

$$10 \times 4$$
$$4 \times 10$$
$$9 \times 4$$
$$10 \times 8$$
$$9 \times 8$$
$$10 \times 9$$
$$9 \times 9$$
$$10 \times 7$$
$$7 \times 9$$
$$6 \times 9$$

Behind the Numbers: How the String was Crafted

The first two problems introduce the commutative property. The array can be turned to help students justify that the factors can be commuted—that the total number of elements in the array is the same. The third problem may be solved in a variety of ways. Some students may double 18, the product of 9×2. If anyone uses the product of the previous problem and subtracts 4, you can remove one cube from each tower to represent the strategy. If no one uses this strategy, you can share it as yours and ask if the students think it works. The next four problems are in pairs to encourage students to make use of ten-times. The last two problems in the string are likely to be challenging and will require considerable discussion about what should be removed from the eighth problem—a group of seven or a group of ten; the same is true of the transition from the ninth to the tenth problems (for which the discussion will concern removing either 7 or 9). This is because the factors have been commuted to press students to think about what is happening. The previous discussion of the commutative property will be helpful now as students work to determine what should be removed in order to solve the final two problems. For additional support, see the related strings that follow—D5 and D6.

Arrays with Connecting Cubes · D5

Distributive and Commutative Properties, Using Ten-Times, Using Partial Products

See D4 for details (page 45).

10×6

6×10

9×6

10×3

9×3

10×7

7×9

7×8

6×9

Arrays with Connecting Cubes · D6

Distributive and Commutative Properties, Using Ten-Times, Using Partial Products

See D4 for details (page 45).

10×7

7×10

9×7

10×8

9×8

10×6

6×9

6×8

Graph Paper Arrays · D7

Distributive Property, Using Ten-Times, Using Partial Products

The previous strings (D4 through D6) employed the use of connecting cubes. Here only graph paper arrays are used. This is another step in the progression towards the eventual use of the open array. Once again the focus is the use of the distributive property of multiplication over subtraction, specifically to use a multiple of ten to figure out a multiple of nine. Do one problem at a time. Use graph paper arrays but display them only after students have explained their strategies. Mark the strategy on the array. For example, if a student says, "I solved 3×9 by subtracting 3 from the 3×10" draw a line with a marker on a 3×10 array to show the new 3×9 array.

3×10

3×9

10×8

9×8

10×7

9×7

6×9

Behind the Numbers: How the String was Crafted

The problems are paired with the ten-times expression commuted and placed first to encourage use of the ten-times strategy. The last two problems in the string are also related. The last one can be solved by making a helper problem or by using the problem before it and removing a group of nine. This last problem also has the factors reversed to challenge students to think about what needs to be subtracted. If this string is easy for your students, you can add two more challenging problems: 20×4 and then 19×4. For additional support, see the related strings that follow—D8 and D9.

Graph Paper Arrays · D8

Distributive Property, Using Ten-Times, Using Partial Products

See D7 for details (above).

10×9

9×9

10×7

9×7

10×6

9×6

6×8

Graph Paper Arrays · D9

Distributive Property, Using Ten-Times, Using Partial Products

See D7 for details (page 47).

$$10 \times 11$$
$$9 \times 11$$
$$10 \times 12$$
$$9 \times 12$$
$$10 \times 9$$
$$9 \times 9$$
$$6 \times 9$$

Graph Paper Arrays · D10

Associative Property, Doubling and Halving

This string of related problems is designed to encourage students to use multiplication facts they know to find answers to other, more challenging ones. The string also supports use of the doubling and halving strategy. Do one problem at a time, giving enough think time before you start discussion. Use graph paper arrays and have scissors handy to cut them to match students' strategies. For example, if a student says, "I cut a 6×8 in half to make a 12×4," cut a 6×8 array into two 6×4 arrays and then place one above the other to make a new array, 12×4.

$$3 \times 4$$
$$3 \times 8$$
$$6 \times 8$$
$$12 \times 4$$
$$24 \times 2$$
$$48 \times 1$$
$$3 \times 16$$

Behind the Numbers: How the String was Crafted

The first three problems are basic facts but they are presented one at a time and related in a way that supports the use of doubling (each one has a factor that is double one of the factors in the previous one). The next three problems in the string are all equivalent since one factor doubles while the other halves. Even if students do not use doubling and halving to produce the answers, the fact that the answers are the same will likely prompt a discussion on equivalence. The doubling and halving is not as easy to see in the last problem. Students must look back over the string to find the problem from which the last one was produced. And since the answer is the same as in the previous four problems, new relationships among the factors can be examined. The associative property underlies the doubling and halving strategy.

A Portion of the Minilesson

Inside One Classroom

Miki (the teacher): *(Writes on the chalkboard 6 × 8.)* Here is the next one…another multiplication fact. What is 6 times 8? C. J.?

C.J.: That's 48.

Miki: *(Writes 48 next to the problem and puts a 6 x 8 array up next to the problem.)* Great, and here's a 6 by 8 array I cut out. Can somebody show us how this is a 6 by 8 array? Megan?

Megan: There's 6 squares going down and 8 going across. *(Points to the rows and columns of the array.)*

Miki: Everybody agrees that we have 6 rows and 8 columns? *(Nods from the class.)* OK, here's another problem. *(Writes 12 × 4 directly underneath the first problem.)* Take a minute to think about how you would solve this problem. When you are ready to share, put a thumb up so you don't disturb other people who are still working on it. *(Waits several seconds before calling on students to share.)* Debbie?

Debbie: Well, I just knew it. I knew 12 × 4 was 48. But I also noticed that it's the same answer as 6 × 8.

Miki: That's interesting, Debbie. Did anybody else notice that? I wonder why that happened.

Claire: I think you double and halve 6 by 8 so it's the same answer.

Miki: Can you say more about that, Claire?

Claire: Well, 12 is double 6 and 4 is half of 8 so the answer is still 48.

Miki: *(Draws an arrow from the 6 to the 12 and from the 8 to the 4 and writes ×2 and ÷2 respectively next to the arrows.)* Claire, can you show us how the doubling and halving works using the 6 by 8 array?

Author's Notes

Learning the basic multiplication facts is critical when moving on to more challenging multiplication problems.

The array provides students with a representation of their strategies. Eventually the array will become a tool with which to think.

One of the reasons that each problem in a string is written directly underneath the previous one is so observations such as Debbie's can be made easily.

Miki asks Claire to expand on her thinking in order to encourage conversation on this important strategy.

continued on next page

continued from previous page

Claire: You cut the 6 by 8 array in half. So you count 4 squares across and cut down the line there. *(Uses scissors to cut the 6 × 8 array in half vertically.)* And then you take one of the pieces and connect it to the bottom of the other piece so that you have 12 squares going down. *(Attaches one 6 x 4 piece to the bottom of the other 6 × 4 piece to make a 12 × 4.)* That's a 12 by 4 array now, and you still have 48.

The paper array is cut and moved to represent Claire's thinking.

Miki: This is interesting. Let's think about the next problem, and how the array can be doubled and halved the way that Claire just did. Here it is: 24 × 2. *(Writes 24 × 2 directly under 12 × 4.)*

Miki invites reflection on the strategy.

Graph Paper Arrays · D11

Distributive Property, Using Partial Products, Commutative Property

This string is composed of related problems designed to encourage students to make use of partial products employing the distributive property of multiplication. Do one problem at a time. Use graph paper arrays and have scissors handy to cut them to match students' strategies, or you can mark the strategy on a previously used array that matches a student's strategy. For example, if a student says, "I solved 6 × 3 by subtracting 6 from the 6 × 4," draw a line on the 6 × 4 array to show the new 6 × 3 array.

$$6 \times 4$$

$$6 \times 3$$

$$3 \times 6$$

$$2 \times 6$$

$$5 \times 6$$

$$8 \times 6$$

$$6 \times 8$$

Behind the Numbers: How the String was Crafted

The first four problems are designed to use the strategies of one group more and one group less. The third problem was produced from the second with use of the commutative property, as a support to help students figure out what to add or subtract. The fifth problem can be solved with the partial products from the third and fourth problems. The sixth can be solved with the fifth and the third. The last two problems revisit the commutative property as a helpful reminder of a way to decide what to remove or add when making helper problems.

Distributive Property, Using Ten-Times, Using Partial Products

This string is composed of related problems designed to encourage students to use the distributive property of multiplication over subtraction, specifically to use a multiple of ten to figure out a multiple of nine. Do one problem at a time. Use graph paper arrays. Display them only after students have explained their strategies. Mark the strategy on the array. For example, if a student says, "I solved 9×3 by subtracting 3 from the 10×3," draw a line with a marker on the 10×3 array to show the new 9×3 array.

$$10 \times 11$$
$$9 \times 11$$
$$10 \times 14$$
$$9 \times 14$$
$$10 \times 9$$
$$5 \times 9$$
$$9 \times 9$$

Behind the Numbers: How the String was Crafted

The problems are paired with the ten-times expression placed first to encourage use of the ten-times strategy. The last two problems in the string are also related. The last can be solved by making a helper problem or by using the fifth problem. If this string is easy for your students, you can add two more challenging problems: 30×9 and then 29×9. The first of these can be used to help with the second (removing nine).

Commutative Property, Doubling, Halving

This string is composed of related problems designed to encourage students to use doubling or halving strategies. Do one problem at a time. Use graph paper arrays and scissors. For example, if a student says, "I solved 3×6 by halving 6×6," cut the array in half to make a 3×6 array. To make an 8×4 when a student says, "I doubled the 4×4" use two 4×4 arrays, placing one above the other.

6×6

3×6

4×4

8×4

8×8

4×8

9×3

6×9

Behind the Numbers: How the String was Crafted

The problems are paired with the relationship of halving or doubling. The first problem in each pair can be helpful for solving the second.

Graph Paper Arrays · D14

Associative Property, Doubling and Halving

This string is composed of related problems designed to encourage students to use a doubling and halving strategy. The associative property underlies this strategy. Do one problem at a time. Use graph paper arrays and cut them or place them together to represent students' strategies. For example, if a student says, "I solved 8×6 by using 4×12. I halved and doubled," cut the array and move the pieces appropriately to show the new array.

10×8

5×8

10×4

20×4

40×2

4×12

8×6

16×3

6×4

Behind the Numbers: How the String was Crafted

The first four problems are related; either doubling or halving will help in solving them. The fourth problem is equivalent to the first. Explore this with the students. The next problem is also equivalent to the first and fourth. The next three problems are clustered to prompt a similar conversation on doubling and halving. Students may simply know the answer to the last problem now, but if not, doubling and halving is a helpful strategy.

The Open Array · D15

Distributive Property, Using Ten-Times, Using Partial Products

This string is composed of related problems designed to encourage students

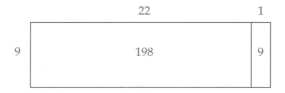

to use the distributive property of multiplication, specifically to use a multiple of ten to figure out a multiple of nine. Do one problem at a time. If you think your students are now comfortable with arrays you can begin to use an open array. For example, if a student says, "I used 9 × 22 and added a 9 to make 9 × 23," you would draw the following:

$$10 \times 15$$
$$11 \times 15$$
$$9 \times 15$$
$$10 \times 22$$
$$9 \times 2$$
$$11 \times 22$$
$$11 \times 23$$

Behind the Numbers: How the String was Crafted

The string is designed with clusters of related problems. The first in each cluster provides the helpful ten-times strategy. The last problem in the string may provide an interesting challenge. What gets added if one uses the prior problem as a helper?

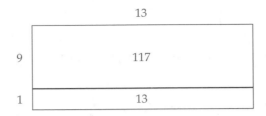

Distributive Property, Using Ten-Times, Using Partial Products

This string is composed of related problems designed to encourage students to use the distributive property of multiplication. If you think your students are now comfortable with arrays, use an open array. For example, if a student says,"I used 10 × 13 and subtracted 13 to make 9 × 13,"you would draw the following:

$$10 \times 13$$
$$11 \times 13$$
$$9 \times 13$$
$$3 \times 13$$
$$13 \times 13$$
$$19 \times 13$$

Behind the Numbers: How the String was Crafted

The problems are all related, in that thirteen is a factor common to all. A variety of partial products in the string can be used to solve the more difficult problems.

The Open Array · D17

Associative and Commutative Properties, Doubling and Halving

This string is composed of related problems designed to encourage students to use the doubling and halving strategy, and to generalize about how factors can be grouped in a variety of ways. Use the open array to model student strategies.

$$10 \times 8$$
$$5 \times 8$$
$$5 \times 16$$
$$20 \times 4$$

$$40 \times 2$$

$$2 \times 2 \times 5 \times 2 \times 2$$

$$9 \times 12$$

$$3 \times 36$$

Can you find some more problems equivalent to 3 × 36?

Behind the Numbers: How the String was Crafted

Except for the second problem, the first five problems are all equivalent in value, and provide students with an opportunity to wonder why this is the case. The second problem is provided as the exception to encourage students to examine factoring, in this case halving. The sixth problem provides all the prime factors of 80 for students to analyze. It is likely that students will group them in a variety of ways and discover that the answer is already in the previous problems. The last two problems in the string are a pair, related to each other by tripling and thirding.

The Open Array · D18

Associative and Commutative Properties, Doubling and Halving

This string is similar to D17. It is composed of related problems designed to encourage students to use the doubling and halving strategy, and to generalize about how factors can be grouped in a variety of ways. Use the open array to model student strategies.

$$6 \times 8$$

$$12 \times 4$$

$$3 \times 16$$

$$24 \times 2$$

$$8 \times 6$$

$$2 \times 3 \times 2 \times 2 \times 2$$

$$10 \times 5$$

$$2 \times 25$$

$$1 \times 50$$

Can you make another problem equivalent to 1 × 50?

Behind the Numbers: How the String was Crafted

The first six problems are all equivalent and provide students with an opportunity to wonder why this is the case. The sixth provides all the prime factors of 48 for students to analyze. It is likely that students will group them in a variety of ways and discover that the answer is already in the previous problems. The last question invites students to consider if all the factors ($2 \times 5 \times 5$) have been used in combinations which appear as problems in the string.

The Open Array · D19

Generalizing the Associative and Commutative Properties

This string is composed of related problems designed to encourage students to generalize about how factors can be grouped in a variety of ways. Use the open array to model student strategies.

$$5 \times 8$$
$$15 \times 8$$
$$15 \times 24$$
$$90 \times 4$$
$$180 \times 2$$
$$60 \times 6$$

Can you find some more problems equivalent to 6 x 60?

Behind the Numbers: How the String was Crafted

The last four problems in the string are equivalent and provide students with an opportunity to wonder why. What are all the factors? Have all combinations been made?

Generalizing the Associative and Commutative Properties

This string is composed of related problems designed to encourage students to use the doubling and halving strategy, and to generalize about how factors can be grouped in a variety of ways. Use the open array to model student strategies.

$$10 \times 6$$
$$5 \times 12$$
$$15 \times 4$$
$$30 \times 2$$
$$60 \times 1$$

Can you find some more equivalent problems?

Behind the Numbers: How the String was Crafted

The problems in the string are equivalent and provide students with an opportunity to wonder why this is the case. What are all of the factors? Have all combinations been made? As students work on the last question encourage them to examine all of the factors and consider grouping them. The associative and commutative properties can be examined.

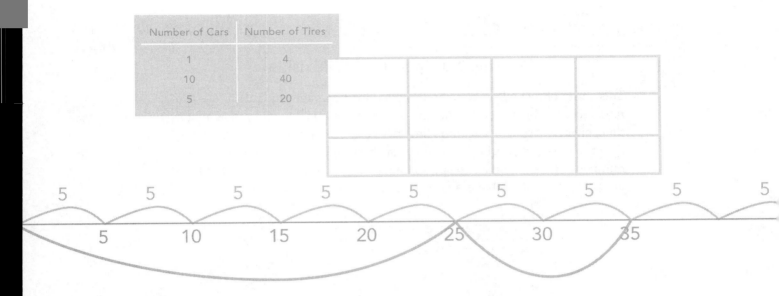

Number of Cars	Number of Tires
1	4
10	40
5	20

Relating Multiplication to Division

All of the models used in the previous sections of this guide can also be used to help students explore the relationship between multiplication and division. The strings in this section are designed to explore how the operations are related. The ratio table, the number line, and the array models are included. You may choose to use the related strings in this section as you work with the models in the previous sections, integrating them and working on multiplication and division simultaneously. Or, you can work with these strings after your students have a deep understanding of multiplication and a comfort level with all three models as a way to extend their understanding of multiplication to division.

Relating Multiplication to Division

This string of related problems is designed to encourage students to use the ratio table flexibly for both multiplication and division. Do one problem at a time, giving students some think time before you start discussion. Presenting the problems in this string in a context, such as a number of cars and the total number of tires they have, helps students realize the meaning of what they are doing. The ratio table is a good model for illustrating such a context.

Number of Cars	Number of Tires
1	4
10	40
5	

10×4

$40 \div 4$

5×4

$20 \div 4$

3×4

$12 \div 4$

$16 \div 4$

Behind the Numbers: How the String was Crafted

The problems in this string have been chosen to encourage students to use multiplication facts they know to solve division problems. The problems are paired to generate a conversation on the relationship between multiplication and division. The last problem requires students to generate the multiplication fact they need to solve the problem. For additional support, see the related strings that follow—E2 through E6.

The Ratio Table · E2

Relating Multiplication to Division

See E1 for details (above).

Number of Tricycles	Number of Wheels
1	3
10	30
5	

10×3

$30 \div 3$

5×3

$15 \div 3$

4×3

$12 \div 3$

$18 \div 3$

The Ratio Table · E3

Relating Multiplication to Division

See E1 for details (page 60).

Number of Hands	Number of Fingers
1	5
10	50
5	

10 × 5
50 ÷ 5
5 × 5
25 ÷ 5
4 × 5
20 ÷ 5
35 ÷ 5

The Ratio Table · E4

Relating Multiplication to Division

See E1 for details (page 60).

Number of Packs	Number of Juice Boxes
1	6
10	60
5	

10 × 6
60 ÷ 6
5 × 6
30 ÷ 6
4 × 6
24 ÷ 6
18 ÷ 6

The Ratio Table · E5

Relating Multiplication to Division

See E1 for details (page 60).

Number of Weeks	Number of Days
1	7
10	70

10×7

$70 \div 7$

5×7

$35 \div 7$

3×7

$21 \div 7$

$28 \div 7$

The Ratio Table · E6

Relating Multiplication to Division

See E1 for details (page 60).

Number of Tickets	Cost
1	9
10	90

10×9

$90 \div 9$

5×9

$45 \div 9$

3×9

$27 \div 9$

$36 \div 9$

The Open Number Line · E7

Relating Multiplication to Division

This string of related problems is designed to encourage students to think of division as jumps on a number line. Do one problem at a time, giving students some think time before you start discussion. It is helpful to present the problems in this string in the context of the length of a jump.

If I make 10 jumps of 4, where do I land?	**10 × 4**
If I'm at 40, how many jumps of 4 did I need to get there?	**40 ÷ 4**
How many jumps of 10 to get to 40?	**40 ÷ 10**
How many jumps of 2 to get to 40?	**40 ÷ 2**
How many jumps of 5 to get to 20?	**20 ÷ 5**
How many jumps of 4 to get to 20?	**20 ÷ 4**

Behind the Numbers: How the String was Crafted

The problems in this string have been chosen to encourage students to use multiplication facts they know to solve division problems. This is developing an important image for quotative division later, as jumps on a number line, and for division as working up to a total (repeated addition), rather than down (as repeated subtraction). For additional support, see the related strings that follow—E8 through E10.

The Open Number Line · E8

Relating Multiplication to Division

See E7 for details (page 62).

If I make 10 jumps of six, where do I land?	**10 × 6**
If I'm at 60, how many jumps of 6 did I need to get there?	**60 ÷ 6**
How many jumps of 10 to get to 60?	**60 ÷ 10**
How many jumps of 2 to get to 60?	**60 ÷ 2**
How many jumps of 5 to get to 60?	**60 ÷ 5**
How many jumps of 3 to get to 60?	**60 ÷ 3**

The Open Number Line · E9

Relating Multiplication to Division

See E7 for details (page 62).

If I make 10 jumps of 9, where do I land?	**10 × 9**
How many jumps of 9 in 90?	**90 ÷ 9**
How many jumps of 10 in 90?	**90 ÷ 10**
How many jumps of 3 in 90?	**90 ÷ 3**

If I make 15 jumps of 6, where do I land?	**15 × 6**
If I make 3 jumps of 30, where do I land?	**3 × 30**
How many jumps of 6 in 90?	**90 ÷ 6**

The Open Number Line · E10

Relating Multiplication to Division

See E7 for details (page 62).

If I make 10 jumps of 7, where do I land?	**10 × 7**
How many jumps of 7 in 70?	**70 ÷ 7**
How many jumps of 10 in 70?	**70 ÷ 10**
If I make 5 jumps of 7, where do I land?	**5 × 7**
How many jumps of 5 in 350?	**350 ÷ 5**
How many jumps of 7 in 14?	**14 ÷ 7**
How many jumps of 7 in 49?	**49 ÷ 7**

The Open Array · E11

Relating Multiplication to Division, Doubling, Halving

This string of related problems provides the number of rows and the total number of squares in an array. Students need to find the number of columns. Do one problem at a time, giving students some think time before you start discussion.

The array has 56 squares and 8 rows.
The array has 56 squares and 7 rows.
The array has 56 squares and 4 rows.
The array has 56 squares and 14 rows. 〉 How many columns?
The array has 56 squares and 2 rows.
The array has 56 squares and 28 rows.
The array has 28 squares and 4 rows.

Behind the Numbers: How the String was Crafted

The problems in this string have been chosen to encourage students to use multiplication facts they know to solve division problems. The problems are related to generate a conversation on the relationship between multiplication and division. The third problem has half as many rows, thus twice as many columns as the first problem. The last problem has half as many squares and the same number of rows as the third problem, with the result that the array in the last problem has half as many columns. For additional support, see the related strings that follow—E12 through E15.

The Open Array · E12

Relating Multiplication to Division, Doubling, Halving

See E11 for details (page 64).

The array has 48 squares and 6 rows.
The array has 48 squares and 8 rows.
The array has 48 squares and 4 rows.
The array has 48 squares and 12 rows.   How many columns?
The array has 48 squares and 2 rows.
The array has 48 squares and 24 rows.
The array has 24 squares and 4 rows.

The Open Array · E13

Relating Multiplication to Division, Doubling, Halving

See E11 for details (page 64).

The array has 36 squares and 3 rows.
The array has 36 squares and 12 rows.
The array has 36 squares and 4 rows.
The array has 36 squares and 9 rows.   How many columns?
The array has 36 squares and 2 rows.
The array has 36 squares and 18 rows.
The array has 18 squares and 9 rows.

The Open Array · E14

Relating Multiplication to Division, Doubling, Halving

See E11 for details (page 64).

The array has 72 squares and 8 rows.
The array has 72 squares and 9 rows.
The array has 72 squares and 4 rows.
The array has 72 squares and 18 rows.
The array has 72 squares and 2 rows.
The array has 72 squares and 36 rows.
The array has 36 squares and 4 rows.

How many columns?

The Open Array · E15

Relating Multiplication to Division, Doubling, Halving

See E11 for details (page 64).

The array has 100 squares and 5 rows.
The array has 100 squares and 20 rows.
The array has 100 squares and 10 rows.
The array has 100 squares and 4 rows.
The array has 100 squares and 25 rows.
The array has 100 squares and 50 rows.
The array has 50 squares and 5 rows.

How many columns?

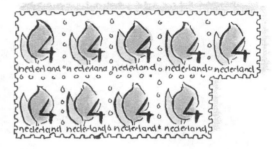

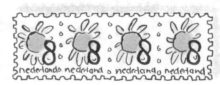

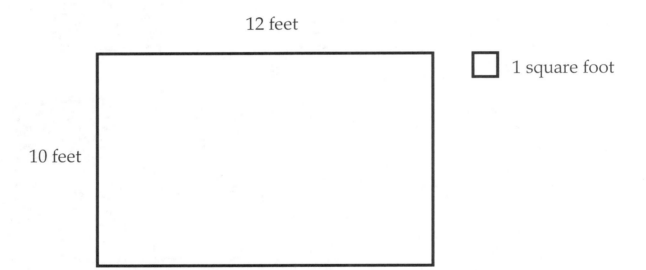

12 feet

10 feet

□ 1 square foot

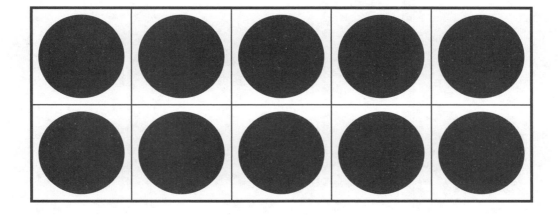

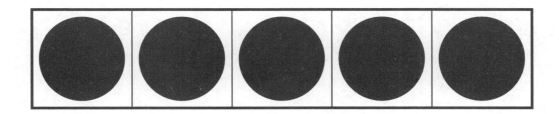